www.finishinglinepress.com

Additional Praise for
QASIDA FOR WHEN I BECAME A WOMAN

QASIDA FOR WHEN I BECAME A WOMAN

New Women's Voices Series, No. 191

poems by

Huma Sheikh

Finishing Line Press
Georgetown, Kentucky

QASIDA FOR WHEN I BECAME A WOMAN

ACKNOWLEDGMENTS

Poems in this book have previously featured in the following journals:

The Cincinnati Review, The Rising Phoenix Review, Solstice Literary Magazine, Downtown Brooklyn: A Journal of Writing, and *The Journal.*

Publisher: Leah Huete de Maines
Editor: Christen Kincaid
Cover Art: Anis Rasheed
Author Photo: Ted Lee
Cover Design: Elizabeth Maines McCleavy

Order online: www.finishinglinepress.com
also available on amazon.com

Author inquiries and mail orders:
Finishing Line Press
PO Box 1626
Georgetown, Kentucky 40324
USA

Contents

This book is dedicated to my father, Ghulam Nabi Sheikh, a professional musician and renowned Ghazal singer of Kashmir, who was killed by Indian police while I was traveling with him. He disappeared during a train journey and was later reported dead by the police, who claimed they had cremated his body almost immediately, in violation of the law requiring a seventy-two-hour waiting period.

This book is also dedicated to my mother, Shakeela Sheikh, without whose unwavering support the completion of this book would not have been possible.

QASIDA FOR ME WHEN I BECAME A WOMAN

"Qasīda is an Arabic ode in praise of a king or nobleman."
—The Qasida, A World Anthology, Translations and introductions by Paul Smith)

Qasida for me when I became a woman
that hot July night when Father's ghost on the bunk
below mine, a caisson rumbling inside me. This
train, sibilance of my feet, air horns at high speed,
between compartments, bathrooms. Father is not here,
Father is not here. The smell of diesel fuel around
me and his nicotine breath an accordion strap,
a memory dragging my shoulder and even as
his voice, melodies in my ears, where are you? Your bunk,
your travel sheet, one crumpled edge hanging off the
frame, a brown towel folded into a pillow
not wanting to smell, not wanting to hear this loss,
sibilance of my feet. Qasida for me when
I became a body possessed of the word rape;
Father killed, daughter raped, this body, sibilance
of my ears, hearing, overhearing, between cries,
whispers a litany of friends, relatives, neighbors—
Father killed, daughter raped by police. Can't I carry
only the weight of the dead, not this rumor-mill:
Father killed, daughter raped? Isn't it enough to survive?
Nobody notices any difference in my face after
I cry. Qasida for me, Huma Sheikh, a writer
of memoirs, because I can walk out in the dark
and feel the moonlight on my face, which is what Sarah
Everard, the thirty-three-year-old woman, must have
felt before her disappearance while walking home
at night in South London, Egyptian women must
be feeling when they can't walk down the night streets
abused by the leering gazes of men, but
I walk out in the dark and scream like that night when
the police lingered outside that train compartment
and one policeman turned the overhead light off, I
need that on because Father is missing, and he
scratched at his arm and stuttered an apology—
that day when I yelled at the judge from the witness

stand; police killed Father, police killed Father and
when our eyes met, he was quick to break it.
Qasida for being left behind, a red mulberry
blessing down my thighs.

QASIDA FOR A WOMAN ON A TRAIN

A Brooklyn subway's screech like Father's last Ghazal
Kam yaar sapidh khwaab jammed into a cassette
recorder
he took around but was not with him
when he died on the Indian train tracks. Now these clinks,
a nickel bowl of a 33rd street fakir,
and his eyes curling around my iced lettuce. My fingers
bleed taco.
Did Father want a bite when he was dying?
Does the fakir taste salsa in my mouth?
A woman's
hip snaps me out of her way. Her swishing skirt
swirls around my thoughts.
How was my father murdered?
His face mutilated?
I and this mystery. Eye and this globe;
the woman's ankles, the nickel bowl, my Father
around the wheels of that Punjab train.

QASIDA FOR PEACE

I want to talk about a honking goose at Lake Ella,
noise, a nuyukha wakes me in my Florida bed
and I wonder what a goose can do
in the Himalayas,
the night sky of war, but pick a mourning, nuyukha,
for men taken by the military and their wives
near sand bunkers
switching babies to their left and right hips,
nuyukha, nuyukha.
I want to talk about the pigeons roosting on rooftops
in the Panhandle but beaks, a basbas, a loop
into caroling a Ghazal; Father's last cry
before his murder.
I want to talk about a sparrow on my windowsill
that digs her breast into my flower vase, flies
off into the deep sky where there are no bars
on the window, Chalo, I say, lets fly above
the backyard hedges, the Hari Parbat peaks
of Kashmir,
the first snowfall in the Himalayas brings
a flying dust of hope, flakes erasing shrapnel.
Sheentral of bullets.
Still, I want to talk about the peace as the honking
goose retreating from her calling into the mountains.

QASIDA FOR MY FATHER'S MUSIC

On a country road in Texas, you sing to me
from the stereo.
Gul phaltum gul yaar chavne,
a memory from our Kashmir home
SYLLABLES floating. A Ghazal. Spring blooms on
the side of the road.
Sunflowers, bare before summer, ooze out
too early. I pull over to the curb on
the Pecos River road,
listen for you, Father
Guu..lu..phel...l..t..e—um, a halting
chime, a soaring death.

QASIDA FOR MY ORCHARD

That looks nothing like a Notre Dame Cathedral
in charred pieces, but a shikara boat seized upon
the shore, how cruel it cannot move across
Jhelum River in a curfew and Kites overhead
lean in for carrion; a silent woman's face
in a houseboat window. How cruel I cannot say
my orchard a shelter broken into 370
pieces, like the law of Kashmir, 370
that used to be mine.

My Orchard, tell me: how do you hear
silence of censored phone lines? It sounds like a belief. Less
precise.Grandma's death prayer inna lillahi rajaoun
when I walk out the door? My ear a sound of a shikara
stroke stretched out, drifting bandaged rib cages, human
hands alongside. My Orchard, do you dream
of freedom, do you dream
that I run past the lingering smoke of grenades
to smell the apples?

QASIDA FOR A FUNERAL PRAYER, FATIHA

In a downpour, the Brooklyn River's motorboat
crushing waves like almonds between teeth.

On this subway some guy punches a door, the crystal
on his finger like Father's coral ring.

Police gave the ring, but not his body
when we reached our destination. Here now, at this Manhattan window,

his shadow my own Fatiha,
inna lillahi wainllahi rajaoon.

QASIDA FOR KEHWA

Sparrows peck at military bunkers as if they are cherries.
A father waits for his son near the bunkers.
Too much saffron hides delicate flavors but it cannot
hide the red and gold graves of children slain.
Mother's Kehwa, she pours into a porcelain cup
alloys the hints of cracked cardamoms against the amber.

QASIDA FOR SAKOON

The Pine trees along the Champions way in Florida
hanging scarves shielding my bowed head that the homeless
man, who asks, where you from? when I pass by his corner
recognizes as neither white, black or native American,
but Cashmere,
exotic and expensive. I say Kashmir and the next day
he says where saffron springs up like weed.
Does he know about the war,
the four seasons, saffron-textured, two neighborhood kids
shot dead
one morning, shrapnel in my right thigh the next evening?

I say India and he says there are many
homeless people there; he raises his cardboard-sign,
HELP, stares at the passers-by, lies on his backpack,
shakes coins in his soda cup. Does he know
about how Muslim marble minarets and Hindu temples
face like war,
the ringing of a Hindu temple bell chasing a Muslim call to prayer?

I sit with him like with the jhuggis and beggars who stole rotis off each
other's hands.
We say nothing.

QASIDA FOR MY MOTHER

I think of Mother hobbling to the shore not on New York's
Oakland Lake where I run and the buses pass.
OM spray painted
on bus stop windows, next to LGBTQ posters.
They might as well be mandalas on telephone poles. Ibadah
Mother would say. I wonder if the boy
who tacked them there
has the same feelings Mother does about the crows on top
of the telephone poles around her house fattened on cumin, staple rice?
Still I can't see her. I run past the Asians, the Hispanics,
the Whites and the Blacks, like a memory's pebble, a bullet skittering
East toward Kashmir's Jhelum,
a war-fed river running down from the mountains,
me strapped on Mother's curving buttocks,
the safe hold of a shikara-boat oar,
splashing past the streams.

QASIDA FOR KANGRIS

That incense of harvest grains in Kashmir,
fresh off the combine, I don't want to recall
because martial boots
chasing the staple breaths
of young men shouting azadi,
each death
a lingering smoke
hung upon each household
like winter coal, burning Kangris
or earthen pots—
in all four seasons.
I let it be.
Love is not a black-brownish cinder
gathered on my windowsill.

QASIDA FOR MY FATHER WHEN POLICE CALLED HIM KASHMIRI SALA

Police call Father Kashmiri sala, bastard,
Kashmiri terrorist. The judge sounds the gavel.
A thousand pigeons watch from the windowsills. Another
day then another then another I walk to the lime-
stone courthouse, a sharp turn, bend, a tree and wall at
war, red and brown leaves over the doorsill. In my dream,
the courthouse is a stone cairn breaking apart. Father,
a grave of pebbles. I am on the witness stand.
The thousand pigeons watch from the windowsills.

QASIDA FOR ONE DAKOTA WINTER

In Vermillion now ungathered flakes
on the window ledge, I listen for a whistle
breeze like military steps marching down
the hardwood floor of that train, Father's skull
clanking against the metal bars. I want
to wander off from Father in the freezing cold.
The sun comes out, I reach to catch. The snow bear
flares like too much vermillion, melting face, eyes.

QASIDA FOR MY FATHER'S GHOST IN MY FLORIDA ROOM

Behind the pine grove, my Panhandle blooms
with rage. I pop pills, walk to last night's chair
where you sat murdered in your blue pathani.
Last night, you bowed your head— never to sing
again, not in the reyaz of our house,
where we laced Ghazals. Last night you bowed
your head, an accordion strap over your shoulder.
Sometimes, I conjure the faces of your
murderers. It begins with your fingers
tapping on the harmonium, tak tak tak tak
until an echo of revenge vibrates
on my fingertips. My eyes can't make you
into clay, can't make a body a body,
again, a heart, a nose, like yours. Your story
didn't flash across the evening news, didn't find
eternity in a Youtube clip. I am six
and feel your shirt against my cheek. I am curling
your hair between my thumb and forefinger,
combing it over your face, laughing.
The palmetto tree in my rear-view mirror

QASIDA FOR WAR

My American friends see nothing that looks
like that girl I was, cherry-dappled cheeks,
fingers curled around Mother's hand, unclenching,
tapping on an elephant bell ringing
in the window. The swinging branches,
ivy penumbra of the days of our siege.
War in Kashmir. A floating flame, a grenade,
from the old kitchen window before a thud,
mirror-like branches in the wind. Mother's
scream-molded silver pots. Father in the mirror.
I pluck my sideburns. My hand, a red vein
reflection of Father's lifetime, glowing in his absence.

QASIDA FOR MY FORMER SELF WHO I MEET
WITHOUT THE BURQA

She tells me Indian soldiers slept
in the neighborhood bunkers, Kashmiri
militants cloaked in pairs in her backyard
hedge. A girlhood in a bullet storm
of her house where joy kicked her little
feet on the bed not a bomb wreck.

Now she surprises me early when
I glimpse her knees. She used to hide
her face in a kameez, hem draped down
on close pressed thighs. Her guarded eyes,
though always full of light, veiled, poetry
at play, unexplored heart in words upon
the page.

She asks me if I deserve
to be in America, not a child
bride in my only knee-length top over loose pants,
kameez and salwar, my house,
my body's awning veil of bricks and mortar.
Now her eyes flirt and spar.
Together, we pour tea.

QASIDA FOR A VISION OF GRENADES
THAT SHAKES LOOSE MY BODY

Of gliding birds in the sky, words out of print.
Kashmir, you taught me to say yes ma'am, no sir,
thank you, even to the middle school teacher
who cut my bangs against my will. Kashmir, your hands,
stroked calm around my bangs. There. There. There.

Your voice like a bitten tongue. Like a misspent grenade.
I breathed through this latest assault.
Kashmir, your swinging Chinar leaves of my childhood,
embers of my hair, even in the summer.

Today, I haul my baggage, press into nearly
empty streets of Florida. The Waffle House
down the road shadowed by Spanish Moss.

The noise of a brown pelican in the sky.

FOR KASHMIRIS, WAR AN EVERYDAY MEAL

Father, no matter what the
glistening visions in blue cosmic wings tell
me, drones soaring in despair in my new
world in Florida's panhandle— my veins, floating wraiths,
spanning the distance, gasping. Today, on the
internet, Kashmiris whipped and kicked. I cry, and mimic
pack animals, carrying identity rugs. How to rebuild
a sense of refuge when hope beans spill and death blooms
for the kin of the slain, memories of dear ones, the
endless crackle of a flesh storm? Kashmir floats with
me, new crises on old ones—a war crumb confetti.
I do the ant's painstaking weight-lifting of fragments.

MOTHER'S VOICE NOT DIPPED IN THE WATER

When she spoke to me on the phone during a flood
her tender breath rose a vibrato floating like
ballooned heads of people drowning the first steps of
the third floor Sister in her arms and eyes closed I
look out my Texas window cars like inflatable
rings around my neck floating a parking lot of
broken houses bare-necks until Mother's voice
blowing dry and braiding Sister and I a grapevine wreath
on the iron-gate of our house.

QASIDA FOR GRANDMA APPAI

At her demise, my mind took the form of a coop
she built in her porch
where girlhood ran in countless circles,
her voice calling out my nickname, happi, happi.

I wonder why memories assume the shape of personal objects,
rigid as stanzas of a formal poem,
yet stitched with the rhythm and meter of breath?
They entangle us as our pelvic region,
each cramp a refrain of the gone past.

Now, five years later, I don't feel those spasms,
yet that pulse on my fingers dial her number.

She lived continents apart and the warm embrace
of her voice
escaped the confines of miles,
boundless like Emily Dickinson's poetry,

I felt a funeral in my brain,
higher levels of iambic tetrameter,
em-dashes harmonizing
Qasidas of recurring clucks.

Huma Sheikh is a poet, essayist, and author born and raised in the war-torn region of Kashmir. Her work bridges personal memory with political conflict, exploring themes of displacement, trauma, and resistance. Her work also explores gender and womanhood. Her writing has appeared in *Kenyon Review, The Journal, Consequence Magazine, Cincinnati Review, Arrowsmith Journal, Solstice Literary Magazine, Prism International*, and others.

She holds a PhD in English with a concentration in Creative Nonfiction and a minor in Poetry, as well as master's degrees in Journalism from the University of South Dakota, English Literature from Texas A&M University, and Creative Writing from Long Island University (Brooklyn). Her memoir *When I Woke Up* was a finalist for the 2024 Black Lawrence Press and Sundress Publications book prizes.

Huma has been recognized with the Adam M. Johnson Fellowship, the Dean's Award for Outstanding Academic Performance, and the Charles Gordone Award for Creative Nonfiction. She has taught writing and literature at Florida State University, University of South Dakota, Texas A&M University, and Long Island University (Brooklyn), and is currently on the faculty at George Mason University and Ohlone College.

www.ingramcontent.com/pod-product-compliance
Lightning Source LLC
Chambersburg PA
CBHW022109080426
42734CB00009B/1527